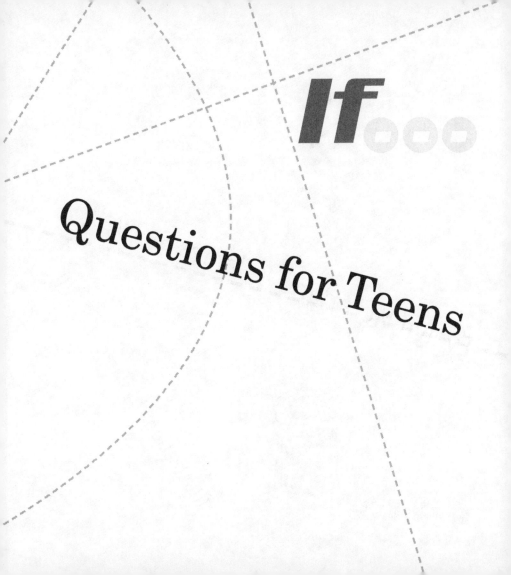

If...

Questions for Teens

Evelyn McFarlane & James Saywell

Illustrations by James Saywell

Villard | New York

If...

Questions

for

Teens

VILLARD BOOKS is a registered trademark of Random House, Inc.
Colophon is a trademark of Random House, Inc.

Library of Congress Cataloging-in-Publication Data
McFarlane, Evelyn.
If—questions for teens / Evelyn McFarlane & James Saywell;
illustrations by James Saywell.
p.   cm.
ISBN 0-375-50555-5 (alk. paper)
1. Teenagers—Conduct of life—Miscellanea.   I. Saywell, James.
II. Title.
BJ1661.M315   2001
081—dc21   00-054647

Villard Books website address: www.villard.com
Printed in the United States of America on acid-free paper
2 4 6 8 9 7 5 3
First Edition

BOOK DESIGN BY BARBARA MARKS

For Giulia and Mackenzie

Special thanks to the following people
for their contributions to this book:
Jen Beier, Jamie Bon, Jenny Campbell, Ann Chow,
Philippine Demeestere, Mallery P. Koons, Mehammed Mack,
Courtney Macken, Luca Ponsi, and Elizabeth Wilson

Introduction

t's either the best period of your life or the worst—usually both. It's either the coolest age to be, or the one you can't wait to grow out of. No one understands you, and too many people seem intent on trying to get you to live your life their way. Our teenage years are some of the most challenging of our lives. But of course they are also great fun. Privacy. Freedom. Respect. Responsibility. Trust. Money. Why won't they give you a bit more? Are you an adult? A kid? A hormonal stew? A future world-saver? All of the above? Love. Looks. Brains. Talent. School. Sports. Piercings. The Web. Music. What's important to teenagers? Anything? Everything equally? Do you know what's going on? Do you know where you're going or where you're coming from? Do you know what kind of person you want to be or what kind of life you want to create for yourself?

If . . . is a book, a game, or even a journal to start you asking questions of yourself, of your best friend, on a date or at a party. Try to guess people's answers first; fill in the margins of the book with your own new questions; send out a juicy one on the Internet and collect great replies; or have your friends write down their answers on the pages to look back on later in life. Make it an adventure!

Who are you?

The world will be yours, so it might be a good idea to find out. And the answers are all there, behind the door that is you. Just inside.

Open it . . .

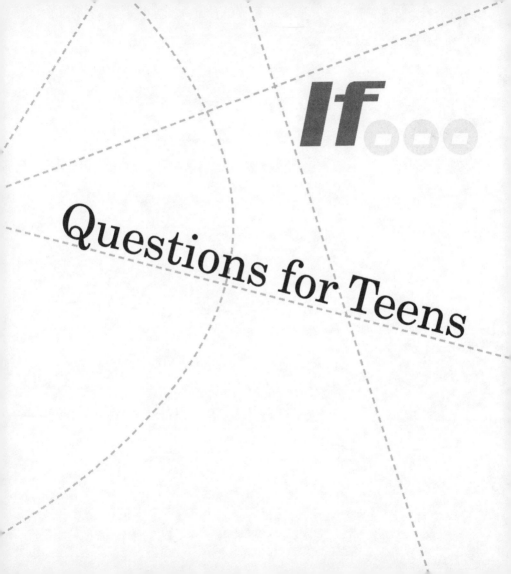

If...

Questions for Teens

f you were to predict what your generation will contribute to the world, what would you say?

f you were to name the person you try to act like the most, who would it be?

f you were to name a belief you hold that is different from that of all of your friends, what would it be?

f there is one mistake you would like your generation not to repeat, what would you say it is?

f you were to describe the ideal after-school hangout, what would it be like and who would you want hanging out there?

HISTORY OF COOL

f you were to name the coolest person in history, who would it be?

f you discovered your boyfriend or girlfriend seriously flirting with someone else, what would you do?

f you were to describe the "perfect" boyfriend or girlfriend, what would you say?

4

I f you could be invited on tour with one rock band or musician, even just to watch every night, which one would you choose to go with?

I f you had an amazing first date tonight, who is the first person you'd tell about it?

I f you could be picked up from school by someone famous, and make sure all your friends could see, who would you choose and how would that person arrive?

I f you were given the money to buy one single thing that would fit in your room, what would you want?

I f you could master one extreme sport, which would it be?

I f there's one way in which people tend to treat you "younger" than you are, what would you say it is?

I f you could hack into one person's, or company's, computer, whose would you break into?

I f you could change one thing about the way your parents act toward you, what would it be?

I f you went shopping with a friend who suddenly started shoplifting something, what would you do?

I f you were to quit school right now and leave home, where would you go and how would you spend your time?

I f your boyfriend or girlfriend wanted to date other people in addition to you, how would you react?

I f you had to name the most unfair thing or decision your parents have ever done or made, what would it be?

7

If someone asked you whether it was better to have older parents or younger ones and why, how would you answer?

If you were to devise a test for picking worthy friends, what would it entail, and what questions would it ask?

If you could have a fast-food restaurant replace your cafeteria at school, which one would you choose?

If you wanted proof of your best friend's loyalty and trust, what would most readily convince you?

If you could make sure that three words were never used on the Internet, which words would you ax?

If you had to predict the worst thing you will witness in your lifetime, what would you say?

If there is one place you'd never want to be seen with your parents, where would it be?

If you were to describe the ways in which boys are more competitive than girls, and vice versa, what would you say?

9

f you could become the ringleader
of any social group at school, which
would it be?

f you could make someone at school
have cosmetic surgery, who would
you transform?

f your mom or
dad asked you
if you've ever
been kissed,
how much
would you tell
them?

f a very close friend of
yours discovered she was
in trouble, and told only you
because she was scared to
tell her parents, what
advice would you give her?

f you could get all the gossip on just one person, who would you choose to know about?

f you had to name the most "male" habit you have, and the most "female" habit, what would you say?

f your website could do anything or be anything, how would it be designed and who would you want visiting it?

f you could keep any one thing in your locker, and have your locker next to that of anyone in your school, what would it be, and who would you want to be next to?

11

f you were in a chat room and decided to lie a bit about yourself, what would you make up?

f you had to give up TV for one year, what would you do with your extra time?

f you could date any member of a boy band or girl band, who would you pick?

f you had to spend a night alone in a haunted house, what three things would you take with you?

If your best friend had a run-in with the law and asked you to lie so he or she could get out of trouble, what would you do?

If you could make your mom or dad listen—*really* listen—to the lyrics of one song that would help them better understand your generation, which song would you choose?

If you had to describe what aspect of your personality makes you most misunderstood, how would you respond?

If you could predict what each of your friends would be doing in ten years, what would you say?

If you were to pick any three friends to go to college with, who would you choose?

If, for fun, you could fix up any two people at school who are real opposites, who would you put together?

If you were to describe the ideal situation for your first kiss, what would you say?

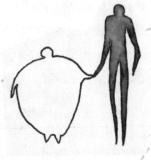

If there's one question that—if asked—you would answer "It's none of your business" to whomever asked it, what would it be?

I f you could change one thing about all the "guys" at school, what would it be?

I f you were going to finish the statement beginning "One thing I'll never let happen to me when I'm older is . . . ," how would you do it?

I f you could change one thing about all the "girls" at school, what would it be?

I f your boyfriend or girlfriend said to you, "Let's go to this party on Saturday and do whatever we both want, with whomever we please, without hurting each other's feelings," how would you respond?

If you were asked to spend a single day at school counseling peers on one issue, what would it be?

If your parents kicked you out of the house right now, where would you go?

If you did not get into any of the colleges that you applied to, what would you do?

If you were to name the one thing that you and your parents will *never* agree on, what would it be?

If you were to state what most teenagers have in common, what would you say?

If you could download completed school assignments from the Internet without getting caught, what would you do?

If one of your teachers came to live with your family for one year, who would you want it to be?

If you had to pick someone on your sports team to be the next U.S. president, who would you pick?

17

I f you could have the sense of humor of any one person at school, whose would you want?

I f you were caught doing something wrong, what would it most likely be?

I f you could put any one thing in someone's locker, what would it be and who would get it?

I f you could understand one person more than you now do, who would it be, and how would you try?

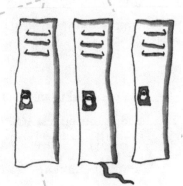

18

f there is one hidden quality you believe you have that you wish people knew about, what would you say it is?

f you were asked to model in a TV commercial for one product only, which would you like it to be?

f you were in charge of planning this year's school formal, where would you want to hold it, and who would be the band?

f you were in the principal's office when he was suddenly called away for a few minutes, and he left all his files open, what would you do?

f someone you liked told you he or she really liked you but didn't want anyone else to know, how would you react?

f you found out by accident that your best friend had a crush on your boyfriend or girlfriend, what would you do?

f you had to say what would be more important than money in your future life plans, how would you respond?

f someone offered you money to pose for photographs without telling you what they would be used for, what would and what wouldn't you do?

f your parents could give you more freedom in one specific situation or area, what would you want it to be?

f there is one person you wish you looked less like, who is it?

f you could tell one of your teachers one specific thing, right to his or her face, and never be punished for it in any way, who would it be and what would you say?

f you were the opposite sex, who, of the people you know, would you like to look like?

If you had to make one thing in the world bigger, what would it be?

If you were to define how much time two people can spend together before they're actually "dating," how would you answer?

If you had to make one thing in the world smaller, what would it be?

If you had to rank your three highest ambitions for your future, what would they be?

I f your parents could make you end one friendship, who do you think they'd choose?

I f you could get advice from any existing call-in radio show, which show would it be, and what would you ask for help with?

I f you were the person chosen to decide the school punishment for cheating on exams, what would you make it?

I f a friend asked you to go someplace you weren't allowed to go, what would you do?

I f you were accidentally locked alone inside your school overnight, but all the rooms were unlocked, where would you snoop?

I f your school offered credit for volunteer work rather than for classwork, what would you think, and what kind of work would you want to do?

I f you were trying to gain the respect of friends, how would you do it?

I f you could magically make one of your teachers suddenly become nude while walking in the hall between classes, who would you cast the spell on?

If you could change
one thing about
MTV, what would
it be?

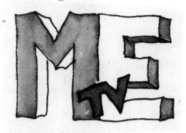

If you started dating
someone two years
younger than yourself,
what do you think your
friends would say?

If you started
dating someone
five years older,
what would your
friends think
about it?

If you had to admit one
thing you envied about
your sister or brother, what
would it be?

If you could have a sports scholarship to any college or university, where would it be?

If there was someone you really liked, but you were too shy to meet on your own, and your best friend knew that person and offered to try to hook you up, what three qualities would you want your friend to say you have?

If you could be more different than your peers, or more like them, in which ways would you change?

If you had to name the one way in which you are most influenced by your peers, what is it?

f you never had to do homework in one subject again, which would it be?

f someone offered you a magic potion that would instantly change you in one way, what would you want it to do, and would you take it?

f you could receive a fair amount of allowance per week, how much would it be?

f you had to honestly rate your looks on a scale of one to ten, how would you come out?

27

If you had to pick the one website that you find most interesting, which would win?

If you had to name the lamest subject you have to study, what would you say?

If you could name one person your age who you think would really benefit from donating some time to volunteer or charity work, who would it be?

If you could make your boyfriend or girlfriend drop one habit, what would it be?

I f you could censor one
thing from the Internet,
what would it be?

I f you could
change one
thing about the
way people your
age treat one
another, what
would it be?

I f you could somehow
embarrass the most
stuck-up person you know,
what would you do
to whom?

I f you gained five pounds
overnight, where would
you like it added?

I f you were to quit school at age sixteen, how do you think your parents would react?

I f you had to pick the experience you will have to face inevitably, that you most fear, how would you respond?

I f you could genetically alter yourself in one way, what would you do?

I f the government were to decide to pay kids money not to do one thing, what would you say it should be?

If you were to have your own website, what would you put on it?

If you had to name the most disturbing or uncomfortable change you went through during puberty, what would it be?

If you were going to be a Big Brother or Big Sister to a kid in your town, how would you spend your time with them?

If you were to name the best change you went through during puberty, what would it be?

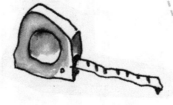

31

If you had to identify the one thing you most look forward to, and the one thing you most dread, about going to college, what would you say?

If you could reprogram television to show more of one thing, what would it be?

If your friends were going to make fun of your crush, what would they most likely pick on?

SHOWERS

If you could secretly spy on one person in the locker room, who would it be?

If you could change
Internet chat rooms in
one way, how would you
make them different?

If you were to name
the best thing and
worst thing about
parties, how would
you respond?

If someone you met in
a chat room wanted
to exchange personal
information about you
or your family, how
much would you
disclose?

If you liked someone
who was either a lot
shorter or much taller
than you are, how
would that affect your
opinion of them?

If you could have any one thing in your backpack at all times, what would it be?

If you had to pick the one person who is nerdy, who you could most easily imagine transformed into a babe, who would that be?

If your buddy asked you for access to your e-mail account, how would you react?

If you noticed that your parents were fighting more often, what would you do?

If you could be school principal for one week, what would you do in the role?

If someone was going to invent an award for Best Teenager of the Year, and asked you to help choose the criteria, what advice would you give?

If your boyfriend or girlfriend still spent time with his or her ex, what would you do?

If you could have one hour per day to call one telephone number for free, what number would it be?

I f you had to predict who in your whole school would turn out to be the biggest success in life, who would it be?

I f you found out that one teacher in your school was secretly a rock musician, who would you guess it was?

I f you could have any singer alive sing at your next party or school dance, who would you pick?

I f you had to name one cosmetic item you couldn't live without, what would you choose?

If you were to predict who, of the girls you know, will become a mother first, who would you pick?

If you could give one of your teachers a raise, and another teacher a pay cut, who would get what?

If a friend of yours—of your gender—made an unexpected pass at you, how would you react?

If you were to predict who, of the girls you know, will get married first, who would you pick?

37

If you witnessed kids picking on someone because that person was different, what would you do?

If you got fired unfairly from your job, and decided to take a bit of revenge on your last day, what would you do?

If you had to live inside a shopping mall for one month, which would be your favorite store?

If you could fix any general problem at school, what would you choose and what would your solution be?

If you could have X-ray vision for one person at school, who would that be?

If you were confused about something related to love, who would you want to talk to?

If you could read all of one person's e-mail, whose would you want to look at?

If you had to retell the silliest thing you ever believed about the opposite sex, before you knew better, what would it be?

39

I f you had to name the worst thing someone you know has done to his or her appearance, what is it?

I f you were going to be sent to boarding school for one year, but had the choice of where it was, where would you go?

I f you had to name the person you know who has recently made the biggest personal transformation, either in appearance, personality, or lifestyle, who would you say it was?

I f you could set the percentage of each race for your school, what would it be?

If your parents told you tonight that they were expecting another child, how would you react?

If you had to describe the biggest difference in your life now from what it was one year ago, what would it be?

If your parents told you tomorrow that they wanted to adopt a child from another country, what would you say?

If you were to name the most important thing you've learned since last year, what would it be?

41

If you had to pick the TV show that has the most realistic teenage characters on it, which one would it be?

If you could dedicate any song on your favorite radio station to one person, what would it be and to whom?

If your parents wanted to take in a foster child who had difficulties, what would you say?

If you could have any new piece of computer equipment, what would you pick?

f you were caught between telling your parents the truth about something and protecting your sibling by lying, what would you do?

f you had to pick your future career right now, and commit to it, what would you choose?

f you had special permission to break one rule, which would you want it to be?

f you had to pick the person you know who would be the most disgusting to kiss, who would you say it was?

If you could be paid money to play one existing video game, which would you prefer to play?

If you were asked to create the perfect summer camp for teenagers, what would go on there?

If you could find the courage to confess one thing to your mom or dad that you have always wanted to, what would it be?

If you had to name what would be the best and worst thing about being left alone at your house for a week while your family went on a trip somewhere, how would you respond?

f you could search the bedroom of one of your friends without anyone—especially your friend—knowing, whose would it be?

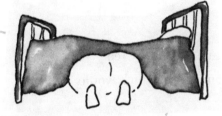

f you could have the entire collection of music from one band, for as long as they recorded, which band would you choose?

f you could make one musician or group permanently retire, and outlaw their music on the radio, who would it be?

f you had to name the age or year when most people seem to "grow up," what would you say?

If you were offered the chance to be part of the first team to colonize another planet, what would you do?

If you could have an hour's free shopping in one store, which would you pick?

If you and your friends were suddenly stranded in the wilderness, who do you think would be the best at survival?

If you could have starred in any music video in history, which would it be?

46

If you found a wallet on the street belonging to someone at school with a lot of cash in it, what would you do?

If one day you woke up with no hair, what would you do?

If you could date one teacher, who would it be?

If you decided to dump your boyfriend or girlfriend, how would you do it?

47

I f you were to be voted
The Most _____ in your
school, what would you
want it to be for?

I f you were voted
The Most _____ in your
school, what would it most
likely be for?

I f you had
to name
the worst
stereotype guys
have about
girls, and girls
have about
guys, what
would you say?

I f you were the owner of a nightclub,
what kind of place would it be, what
would you name it, and what kind of
music would you feature?

If you had to wear a uniform to school, but you could design it, what would it look like?

If you were the official censor for music lyrics, how strict would you be?

If you were to pick the dumbest thing that teenagers in general spend money on, what would it be?

If you and your close friends secretly agreed to start your own fashion trend, what would it be like?

f you were cloned, what would you have your clones do?

f you had to recall one time when you wished your parents had asked your advice before they did something, when was it?

f you had to choose which of your current teachers is the cutest, who would you pick?

f a fortune-teller told you that you were destined to be very famous someday, what would you guess it would be for?

If your school allowed you and only you to open a part-time store inside the school, what would you sell?

If you wanted to make your boyfriend or girlfriend a little bit jealous, how could you do it most effectively?

If you could add one facility to your school, what would it be?

If you could have one person in school come up to you in front of everyone else and ask you out for a date, who would you want it to be?

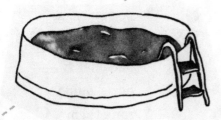

If you had to play on one sports team of the opposite sex, and be the only one of your gender on the team, which sport would you choose?

If you were being interviewed for a summer or part-time job and were asked to give the most important reason why you should be hired, how would you answer?

If you had to place in order of importance the following attributes—intelligence, looks, hipness, talent, humor, personality—how would you rank them?

If you could give one piece of advice to a teen whose parents have recently been divorced, what would you say?

52

If there is one experience you've had that you wish you'd been older for, what would you say it was?

If you noticed that your best friend was flirting with one of your parents, how would you react?

If you could snap your fingers and change one single thing about your face, what would you choose?

If, in biology, the teacher announced that the class would dissect one student, who would you vote be used as the subject?

53

I f there is one award at graduation you lust after, which is it?

I f you were starting a new secret club, what would you invent as the initiation ritual?

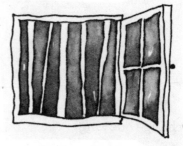

I f you were at a party and needed a ride home, but the only person who could give you a lift was a terrible driver who made you feel unsafe, what would you do?

I f you were to propose one solution to end violence among teenagers, what would it be?

If you had to pick which of your friends has the worst taste in girls or guys, who would you say it is?

If you were going to stop listening to music for one whole year in exchange for an amount of money, how much would it take?

If your best friend asked to borrow all your savings, how would you respond?

If you had to name your biggest disappointment so far, with regard to dating and romance, what would it be?

I f you had to guess what percentage of cell phone calls that teens make is actually necessary, what would you say?

I f you had to name the decision you most dread making but know you'll eventually have to, what would you say it will be?

I f your parents were going to punish you by sending you to spend the summer with one person or in one specific place, who or where would be the worst?

I f you decided to go into professional wrestling, what would you call yourself, and what would you wear in the ring?

56

I f you decided to cheat on a test of 100 questions, how many would you have to cheat on before you felt guilty?

I f your parents were going to punish you by denying you something, what would be most effective?

I f you had to describe your idea of the perfect first date, how would it go?

I f you were asked whether an Internet relationship is cheating on your boyfriend or girlfriend, what would you say?

f a good friend asked you to help cheat on a test he or she would otherwise fail, what would you say?

f there is one person you know who makes you feel uncomfortable, who is it?

f you found out that one of your friends "borrowed" a bit of an assignment you wrote, how would you react?

f you had to name the person at school who is most comfortable talking about any subject in the world, who would it be?

If you were to name the cutest person at school, what would you say makes them so?

If you were to pick the song whose lyrics best describe your life right now, what song would it be?

If you knew right now that you would inherit a fortune in ten years, how would you live your life differently?

If you were going to define the term *normal* as it relates to people you know, what would you say?

f you were to describe the type of boy or girl you are attracted to, how would you do it?

f you were to pick the dumbest thing your parents spend money on, what would you say it is?

f you could have your parents trust you more in one specific area, what would it be?

f you had to pick one bad thing that you feel certain will happen to you during your lifetime, what would you say it will be?

60

I f you were asked where you think kids learn their worst character traits, how would you respond?

I f you were going to start a gang, what would you call yourselves?

I f you were to pick one person you know whose success continually bugs you, who is it?

I f a movie producer wanted to make a new film about someone truly evil and someone truly saintly, and asked you to suggest two people you know as examples he could study, who would you nominate?

If you had to define the difference between a girl and a woman, in words or by using an example, how would you do it?

If you had to define the difference between a boy and a man, how would you answer?

If your favorite band wanted to use an existing photo of you for its next CD cover, which one would you give them?

If you were offered one free cosmetic operation of your choice, which would you choose, if any?

If you died tomorrow, what one thing would you say had made your life so far worth it all?

If you could have a great talent, what would you want it to be?

If you had to die a death so dramatic that no one would ever forget it, how would you die?

If you had to admit what you envy most about your worst enemy, what would it be?

63

If you had to name your worst personality flaw, what is it?

If you had to name the lamest video on MTV right now, which would you say it was?

If you had to name the single cutest thing about your boyfriend or girlfriend, what would you say?

If you had to choose between being voted most popular, most beautiful, smartest, best athlete, or most likely to succeed in life, which would make you happiest?

If the school yearbook decided that this year students would have three words listed under their photos, and nothing else, what three words would you choose for yours?

If you could dance as well as one person you know, who would it be?

If you were to remember the one time when you most quickly improved at one thing, when was it?

If you had to name the most overused word among your age group, what would you say?

65

If you had three angels, what would you put each one in charge of?

If you were to say what aspect of being a teenager makes you feel most alone, what would it be?

If you could confront the adult world on one issue, what would it be?

If you were to name the one person you know who has the most "normal" family life, who would it be and what makes it so?

If you had a relative who could get you into a college that otherwise would never accept you, what would you do?

If you were to name the friend who commands the most respect from you and others, who would it be?

If your parents had you when they were quite a bit younger or older, how do you think your life would have been different?

If you found yourself at a party in a house where the owner kept a gun, how would you feel about it?

f one of your teachers winked at you, what would you do?

f your school wanted to invite the smartest person in the world to speak to a student assembly or graduation, who would you nominate for the honor?

f you walked into the bathroom at school and saw a good friend of yours doing an imitation of you, what would you do?

f you walked into the school bathroom and saw a friend of yours drinking something you didn't recognize, what would you do?

If you were to give up freedom in one area of your life in order to have more in another, what would you choose for each?

If you could have the life of one star from a television series, whose would you pick?

If you were to name the one thing you look forward to most about finishing school, what would you say?

If you could have worked for any Internet company when it first started, which would you have chosen?

f you could magically make your boyfriend or girlfriend change the way he or she acts with you in one specific way, what would you want it to be?

f you discovered that your boyfriend put makeup on, how would you feel about it?

f your girlfriend asked you how she should change her makeup, what would you say?

f you had to pick the one thing you are relatively sure will happen to you that will be good, what would you say?

f the police came to you and asked you to report on the activities of a friend, how would you react?

f you were baby-sitting a real brat, what would you do to maintain control?

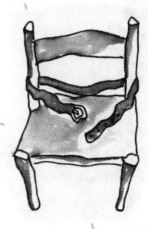

f while baby-sitting at a neighbor's, you discovered something really weird in the house, what would you do?

f you were to base your existence on one thing, what would you say it was?

If you could name the one thing you wake up for in the morning, what would it be?

If you were to name the biggest "sleazes," both male and female, in your school, who would take the honors?

If you could be accepted at any college or university in the world, which would you choose?

If you could have anyone kicked out of school, who would go?

72

If you could get your parents off your back about one thing, what would it be?

If you had to either give school authorities damaging information that would get a friend suspended or take the rap yourself, what would you do?

If you ended up having to take care of a child while you were still in high school, who do you think you would turn to most for help or advice?

If you were approached on a bus by a stranger who was acting odd, what would you do?

73

If you had to say in one word or phrase what you hope to get out of your future career, how would you answer?

If you could take one year off from school, without worrying about money, what would you spend it doing?

If you came upon a really cool car, with its motor running but no one around, and knew you could "borrow" it for a joyride, what would you do?

If a rich uncle you didn't even know sent you a thousand dollars and said, "Have fun with it!," what would you do?

f you were going to help the person you know with the worst identity problem, who would it be and how would you help?

f you had to marry someone you know at school right now, who would you pick?

f you could change one thing about your eating habits, what would it be?

f there were such a thing as a Truth About Everything club, in which members would have to say exactly what they knew or thought about one another, and you were invited to join along with your friends, what would you do?

I f you could
teach your pet
to do any one
thing on
command that
it cannot do
now, what
would it be?

I f you and three close friends
got backstage passes for a
concert, but once there found out
that only three of you could go
in, what would you do?

I f there was to be one
class period each
week devoted to
something practical
and useful in life, what
should it be?

I f you could predict what
your best friends will be
when they grow up, what
career would you pick for
each of them?

I f you had to guess what the opposite sex of your age group talk about most when they get together, what would you say?

I f you had to name the best kisser, who would it be?

I f you had to confess what you envy most about your best friend, what would it be?

I f you found out that one of your closest friends was flirting with a teacher, how would you react?

If one of your close friends admitted to you about feeling uncomfortable with his or her stepmother or stepfather but asked you not to say anything to anybody, what would you do?

If you were to name a family whose home habits you find either embarrassing or downright weird, who are they?

If you had to describe the worst thing your best friend could do to you, how would you answer?

If you were invited to dinner at the White House and had to bring a date who wasn't your boyfriend or girlfriend or a relative, who would you ask?

If you were to name the nicest thing your best friend has ever done for you, what would you say it was, and how did you thank them?

If there is something you'd feel more comfortable asking or discussing with a stranger on the Internet than discussing with your parents or friends, what would it be?

If you were going to offer an example to explain "peer pressure" as you have witnessed or experienced it personally, what would you cite?

If you were to say in what aspects teens, in general, are most cruel to one another, how would you answer?

If you were to become a doctor, what would your specialty be?

If you had to pick one thing you hope happens to you more than anything else before you turn twenty, what would you say it is?

If you had to describe the differences between the kind of friends your parents would prefer you to have, and those you do, what would you say?

If there is one thing or experience you really hope you can avoid until *after* you turn twenty, what is it?

If your friends were to accuse you of trying to look like someone famous, who would it most likely be?

If someone asked you whether parents should "reward" their kids for good behavior or grades, how would you respond?

If your parents offered you a reward to finish the year with better grades, what would you ask for?

If you were to name the one thing you most admire about your parents, what would you say?

81

I f you could
sail around
the world with
three people,
who would you
want them
to be?

I f you had to name the
friend with the most
bizarre eating habits,
who would it be?

I f you wanted to get the kids you know of
your age group together to protest
something, what is the most obvious thing
you'd be against?

I f you could prevent one friend from
dating someone in particular, who
would that person be?

82

f you had to relate your most embarrassing moment in life so far, when was it?

f there was one thing you think every kid should be warned about with regard to being a teenager, what is it?

f on a first date you were trying to impress someone with your accomplishments or attributes, what would you brag about first?

f your bedroom had a special window onto anything in the world, inside or outside, what would it look out on?

f you could snap your fingers and become either a genius brain or a beauty god, which would you go for, and how do you think your friends would treat you afterward?

f you had to describe the dumbest thing you ever did on a date or at a party, what was it?

f you could do one specific thing for the environment, what would it be?

f you were really attracted to someone you saw at a party, what would your strategy be to get to know that person?

I f you had to pick a moment in your life when things turned for the worse, and a moment when things turned for the better, what would they be?

I f you were to change your hair color, what would you make it?

I f you were to say whether you are more attracted by looks, brains, or personality, what would you say?

I f your parents promised they would find the money for any college you could get into, what effect would it have on your school attitude or efforts?

If you could have one phone conversation with the president of the United States, what would you want to talk about?

If you could give a prize for the coolest person in your school, who would win?

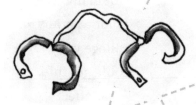

If you could give a prize for the biggest jerk in your school, who would take it, and what would the prize actually be?

If, on a first date, the girl or guy you were out with acted too forward and aggressive physically, but you still really liked that person, what would you do?

If you had to estimate whether the average teenage guy thinks more about girls, sports, or food, what would you say?

If you could visit any website, watch any movie, or see any TV show without your parents intervening, what would you choose?

If you had to admit your most embarrassing makeout moment, what would it be?

If you could undo one tattoo or piercing on yourself or someone you know, which would it be?

If you could crowd surf any one of your teachers, who would you choose?

If you had to name the worst sin you'd be capable of committing, what would you say it is?

If you were going to talk to a therapist in private, what's the first thing you'd want to talk about, and what do you think the most difficult thing to talk about would be?

If you could tell off one adult person you know, and not get in trouble for it, who would it be, and what would you say?

I f you found out that your dad worked in the Mafia, how would you react?

I f you had to write a law giving the youngest legal age of consent for getting married, what would that be?

I f you discovered by accident that one of your parents was a spy, how would you feel about it?

I f you were to name the biggest difference between how your guy friends feel about girls, and how your girlfriends feel about guys, what would you say?

f you were to name someone whom body piercing suits most, who would you pick?

f your sibling found out you were surfing stuff on the Web that you weren't allowed to, what would you say to persuade your brother or sister to keep the secret?

f you had to name the single most difficult situation or problem you've ever faced as a teenager, what would it be?

f you were to imagine the worst situation you could ever face, what would it be?

I f you had to name the most annoying question your best friend asks, what would it be?

I f you wanted to play a practical joke on a teacher without getting caught, what would you do?

I f you were to consider the person you know who is the most messed up, what would you say is the main cause of his or her trouble?

I f one famous athlete were to ask you for advice on how to play even better, who would you want it to be, and what would you advise?

If you could evict one sports star from sports, who would you expel?

If you had to name the one nonrelative you trust most in the world, who would win the honor?

If you were going to get a tattoo, where would you put it, what would it be, and how would your parents react?

If you had to predict who, of your current friends, will contribute most to the world in the future, who would get your vote?

If you could make one person you know live as *you* for one day, and do all the normal things you do, in order to understand you better, who would you choose?

If you invented a new video game, what would it be like?

If you had to choose one type of music that best represents your personality, what would it be?

If you met someone on the Internet and he or she wanted to meet you in person, what would you say?

If you were to name your best and worst sports moments, what would they be?

If you were to name what, to you, would be the sweetest victory possible, what would you say?

If you could have the world's largest collection of one thing, what would you choose?

If you could wear anything you wanted to work, but it had to be exactly the same every day, what would you wear?

If you were put in charge of programming for MTV, how would you run it?

If you could have kept one thing secret from your parents and one thing secret from your friends, something they now know about, what would it have been for each?

If you could secretly get a message to someone you like, without that person knowing who sent it, how would you do it and what would it say?

If you were to choose your hippest teacher, who would it be?

If you had to name one negative experience that you are glad you went through anyway, what was it?

If all your good friends planned a weekend without you, how would you react and what would you do?

If you had to name the area of your life in which you need more confidence, what would you say it was?

If you had a secret crush on someone, and you could tell that person one thing without becoming embarrassed, what would you say?

If there is one thing that you're totally sick of hearing from older people, what is it?

If you could jump forward to any time in life, to what point would you go?

If your dad or mom were asked to be school principal this year, what would you advise them to do?

If you had to put in order of importance the following qualities for a friend—honesty, loyalty, generosity, sense of humor—how would you do it?

If you were to name the most together person you know in your age group, who would it be?

If you could be liked more by any one person, other than romantically, who would you want it to be?

If your best friend asked you to help him or her break a terrible habit, how would you go about it?

If you could write tomorrow night's newscast so that three wonderful bits of international news would happen, what would they be?

f you had to name the best and worst diets you've ever tried, what would you say?

f your younger sister or friend asked you to tell them what unsafe sex is, and what safe sex is, how would you answer?

f you could fix your best friend up with one person you know, who would it be?

f you had to pick one well-known person who should be a role model for teenagers today, who is it?

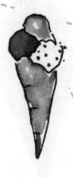

If you discovered that something was missing from your room, who is the first person you'd suspect?

If you could empower teenagers in any one way, what would it be?

If one item of food were going to be made permanently available for free to everyone, what would you want it to be?

If you had to relive one year of school, which year would you repeat?

100

If you had to imagine the worst person to date, who would you say it was?

If you were trying to impress a really cute guy or girl, how would you do it?

If you were to name the coolest person you know who's over thirty, who would it be?

If your best friend asked your advice on how to be more popular, what would you say?

If you were to name the hardest thing you ever had to tell someone, what was it?

If you could pick where your class went on its next field trip, where would it be?

If you could have a secret date with the older brother or sister of one of your friends, who would it be?

If you were to predict who, of the people you know, will turn out to be famous before they turn thirty, who would you pick and what will they be known for?

f you could be paid money for doing one thing, what would it be?

f your boyfriend or girlfriend told you he or she had videotaped you when you didn't know it, how would you feel?

f one hour into a first date you were totally bored, what would you do?

f you could be any other age right now, how old would you choose to be?

If it were up to you, how available would you make condoms in school?

If you could win an Oscar, an Emmy, a Tony, a Grammy, or a Webby, which would you want most?

If you could be the on-air host of any call-in radio show, what kind would it be?

If you could enforce one new rule in your school, what would it be?

If you could have one particular dish added to your school cafeteria menu, what would it be?

If you could own any one of your friends' CD or video collections, whose would you want to have?

If you were to name the coolest thing you've ever come across on the Internet, what was it?

If you had to name the most common way most teenagers are misunderstood, what would you say?

105

f you could secretly learn another language, and no one would know you understood it, which would it be?

f you were to choose who has the coolest parents, among people you know, who would it be?

f you were invited to be a backup singer for any band, which would you want it to be?

f you had to name one school grade you got that was truly unfair, which was it?

f your friends wanted to surprise you with one guest at your birthday dinner, who do you think they'd pick?

f you wanted to bug your mom, how could you best do it?

f your mom wanted to bug you, what's the best way she could do it?

f you could have a collection of all the episodes of one television series, which would it be?

I f you were to name one person who defines the term "two-faced," who would you say it is?

I f the boyfriend of your best friend or your sister started flirting with you, what would you do?

I f you wanted to ask someone new out for a date, how would you word it?

I f someone who had recently made you really angry now wanted your forgiveness, what would that person have to say or do?

f you had to name the most disgusting thing a friend ever did, what would you say?

f you wanted people at school to think of you as more macho, or more feminine, what would you need to do?

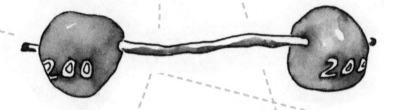

f someone was being picked on at school by people you are a bit frightened of yourself, what would you do?

f teenagers knew a special language that no one else could understand, how would life be different?

If your older sister or brother agreed to lend you one thing whenever you wanted it, what would you pick?

If there were three words you think your generation could claim as its own, which would you say they are?

If you had to imagine the most embarrassing thing that could happen to you while with your family, what would it be?

If in school every student was given a computer and allowed one hour a day of class time to surf the Web, what do you think most students would surf for?

If you had to confess the one thing about yourself that would most embarrass you if people or friends found out about it, what would it be?

If you were to pick the people you know who are best and worst at hiding their emotions or feelings, who would they be?

If you could talk on the phone as long as you wanted to every day, how long would it be?

If your younger siblings asked you, based on their personalities, what you thought they should major in, what would your answer be?

If you could have more time each week for sports, sleep, Internet surfing, TV, or your boyfriend or girlfriend, which would you choose first?

If there was one thing you wished you *didn't* know about your boyfriend or girlfriend, what is it?

If you could know one juicy thing about your boyfriend or girlfriend, what would it be?

If you had to name the bravest thing you've ever done for a friend, what was it?

f all your friends got together and decided to take revenge on one horrible person in school who deserved it, what would you do and to whom?

f you had to name the one person you know whose body you'd like to have, who is it?

f you had to name your biggest fear regarding your parents, what would you say it is?

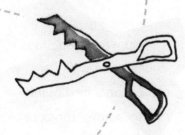

f you could have any body you want, what would it look like?

f you were to pick the two most important things you'd want in a boyfriend or girlfriend, what would you say?

f there was one gift you got recently, and you'd *really* rather have had the cash, what was it?

f you were to pick the two most important things you'd want in a husband or wife, what would they be?

f you were going to get either a new TV, a new computer, a new mobile phone, a new stereo, or a new PlayStation for your next birthday present, which would you choose?

114

I f you saw someone you work with, but didn't know too well, stealing something from work, what would you do?

I f your dad gave you his car for a day, to go wherever you wanted with it, where would you go?

I f your best friends asked you to honestly tell them how they did in the school play, or some similar display of their talents, and they really stunk, what would you say to them?

I f one of your friends told you he or she had a crush on one of your parents, who do you think it would most likely be, and how would you react?

If on the night before the school yearbook was printed, you could substitute something under the picture of one person, who would you choose, and what would you write?

If you had to pick the one time when a friend hurt your feelings the most, when was it?

If you had to classify teenagers into four basic types, what would they be and which group would you put yourself in?

If you hooked up with a stranger on e-mail, what three questions would you ask to see if you were compatible?

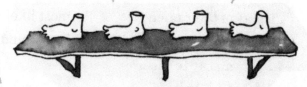

If you could quit school at any age you wanted, how soon would you?

If you could drink legally, how often would you do it?

If you had to pick the movie you've seen that had the coolest trailer but was most disappointing in full length, which was it?

If you had to go to school on Saturday mornings, but it could be to study one thing that you don't right now, what subject would you choose?

If you had to remember the best, most original, and cleverest excuse you've ever come up with to get out of doing something, what was it?

If you could entirely skip any one grade of school, which would you choose to miss?

If a guy or girl you liked asked you out, but you knew that your best friend really liked that person a lot, what would you do?

If you were at a party and everyone decided to play truth or dare, who in the world would you be most scared of playing with?

If a great-uncle you never knew about died and left you in charge of distributing $100,000 among your family, how would you distribute it?

If you had to pick the worst moment of each day at school, what would you say?

If you could play any music during dinner each night, what music would you put on?

If you could get over being envious of any one thing, what would it be?

I f you were to be an exchange student somewhere, where would you want to go?

I f you wanted to be really nasty and start a rumor about someone to make that person less popular, what would you say, and about whom?

I f someone started a false rumor about you, which kind would make you the most upset or nervous?

I f you could be exempted from one phys-ed activity forever, which would it be?

If you were to go into sales, what would you be able to sell best?

If you could sneak into the school records to change the final grade of one student—not yourself—who would it be, and which way would you change it?

If you heard that cell phones fry brain cells, how seriously would you take it?

If you could arrange for two music stars to get married, who would they be?

f you could have
been the first person
to do any single thing,
what would it be?

f you suspected
someone you knew
only on the Internet of
lying about age or
gender, what would
you ask to try to find
out the truth?

f you could have told
off any one friend
but didn't, who would
it be, and for what?

f you had to name the one
thing you'd most hate
your parents to walk in on
you doing, what is it?

f you had to have dinner with one sports figure, who would you pick who you think would be the most interesting person to talk to when *not* discussing sports?

f you found out you were related to one famous wrestler, who would you want it to be?

f your parents surprised you tomorrow morning by announcing that they were sending you to military school, what would you say to them?

f you had to name the cruelest kind of behavior inflicted on someone at school other than yourself, what was it and to whom was it directed?

If you were to name one person who defines the word *loser* or the word *winner,* who would it be?

If you had to confess the main way in which you succumb to peer pressure on a regular basis in your everyday life, what would it be?

If you were going to cite one way in which you resist peer pressure, what is it?

If you were asked whether you have a different standard for acceptable dating behavior for boys than for girls, what would you answer?

If you had to define what action would make you dump your boyfriend or girlfriend immediately with no going back, what would it be?

If your school was considering installing metal detectors at all entrances, how would you feel about it?

DO NOT CROSS

If you had to guess up to what point your girlfriend or boyfriend would forgive you, but beyond which you'd break up, what is it?

If you were going to rush up to one person in the hall at school and plant a kiss just to see how she or he would react, who would you choose?

125

If there was one person you know who you wish would lose a bit of weight, but you don't have the courage to say anything, who would it be?

If you were asked to pick someone who would become the physical type all kids of your gender aspired to, who would you select?

If you could ask the closest friend of your boyfriend or girlfriend one question, knowing you would get the truth, what would you ask?

If you were to pick one fashion idea that doesn't seem fair to real people with real bodies and faces, what would you say it was?

If there was one famous sports figure you wish would be taught a lesson in humility, who would you name?

If your country suddenly entered a war in another country that you didn't know much about, and volunteers were needed badly, what would you do?

If you had to list the worst and best things about being a teenager, how would you answer?

If you had to name the thing you will miss most about being a teenager, what would you say?

f you have an interesting or humorous question or answer to contribute to sequels of *If* . . . , we would love to hear from you. Please send your response or new question to the address below. Please give us your name and age, and sign and date your contribution. Thank you.

Evelyn McFarlane
James Saywell
c/o Villard Books
299 Park Avenue
New York, NY 10171

E-mail: author@ifbooks.com
Website: www.ifbooks.com

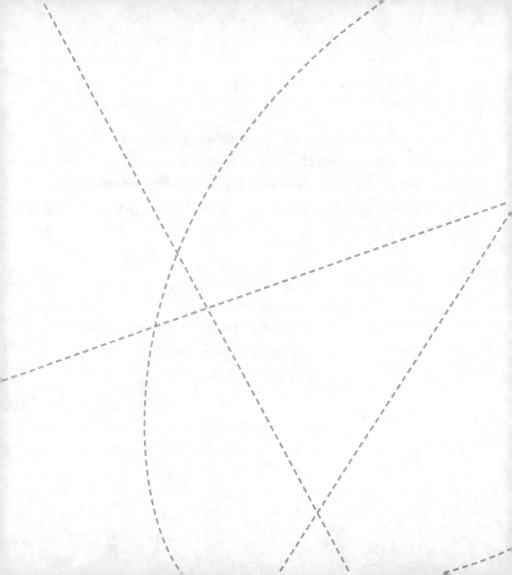

About the Authors

VELYN MCFARLANE was born in Brooklyn and grew up in San Diego. She received a degree in architecture from Cornell University and has worked in New York and Boston as an architect. She now lives in Florence, Italy. In addition to writing, she lectures on architecture for the Elderhostel programs in Florence and paints, and is now enjoying the adventure and joy of motherhood.

AMES SAYWELL was born in Canada and lived in Asia as a child. He writes books in Italy and designs furniture in Hong Kong.